The French Connection

by Sharon Franklin

Scott Foresman
is an imprint of

Glenview, Illinois • Boston, Massachusetts • Chandler, Arizona
Upper Saddle River, New Jersey

Photographs

Every effort has been made to secure permission and provide appropriate credit for photographic material. The publisher deeply regrets any omission and pledges to correct errors called to its attention in subsequent editions.

Unless otherwise acknowledged, all photographs are the property of Pearson Education, Inc.

Photo locators denoted as follows: Top (T), Center (C), Bottom (B), Left (L), Right (R), Background (Bkgd)

Cover Gary Paul Lewis/Shutterstock; **1** sbphotog/Fotolia; **5** Getty Image/Thinkstock; **7** marinaphoto/Fotolia; **8** Ivan Cholakov/Shutterstock; **9** (B) Douglas Tomko/Fotolia, (T) Ilene MacDonald/Alamy; **10** Ian Dagnall/Alamy Images; **12** Andre Jenny/Alamy Images; **13** rudi1976/Fotolia; **14** ©G.E. Kidder Smith/Corbis; **15** Adam Jones/Danita Delimont/ Alamy Images; **16** (B) Gary Paul Lewis/Shutterstock, (T) sbphotog/Fotolia; **17** Nathan Benn/Alamy Images; **18** Jackie Smithson/Shutterstock; **19** Exactostock/SuperStock; **20** Biosphoto/SuperStock; **21** ©Royalty-Free/Corbis; **22** rSnapshotPhotos/Shutterstock.

ISBN 13: 978-0-328-51421-2
ISBN 10:   0-328-51421-7

TABLE OF CONTENTS

Introduction

Are you ready for a big adventure? Read about my visit to places in North America that began as early French settlements. Yes, French!

You will learn how French history and culture still have a lasting **influence.** You'll also see how places have changed since their early French beginnings.

I recorded my trip using journal writing, photos, video, picture postcards, and an interview. I visited five places, starting in Canada and then heading south.

Are you ready? Let's go!

The red dots mark the places I visited.

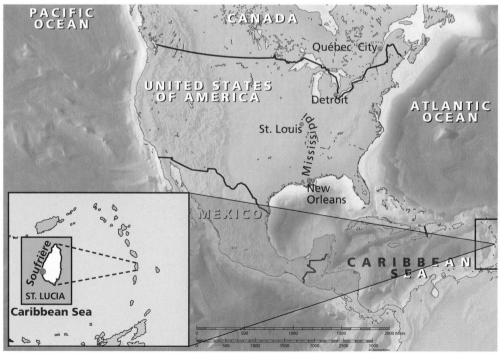

Chapter 1   Québec City, Québec, Canada

Long before the British arrived, the French began exploring North America. As early as 1535, Jacques Cartier explored the St. Lawrence River. In 1608, Samuel de Champlain founded the first permanent French colony.

The colony was on the St. Lawrence River channel, at a place called Quebecq. The name came from an Algonquin word meaning "the place where the river narrows." The colony grew, and soon it became the center of New France. By the time the British took control of the colony in 1759, it was known as Québec City.

Québec is the only fortified city north of Mexico.

Journal

Tuesday, June 3

Although Québec City is in Canada, it sure feels French to me. It is known as the heart of French culture in North America. Many people are **bilingual**—they speak both English and French. However, the majority of people speak mostly French.

Wednesday, June 4

The colony began by the river. Today that part of Québec City is called the Lower Town. I could almost see the people fishing and the merchants doing business there in the city's earliest days. To take over Canada in the old days, you had to get to Québec City first. In fact, between 1629 and 1775, the city was attacked five different times! So, both the French and the British built **fortified** walls around the upper part of the city. It is called Upper Town.

I took a three-mile walk around the wall. Then I hiked down to the Lower Town by way of a steep, winding street.

Thursday, June 5

Today, I visited two places. First, I went to the Fairmont Le Château Frontenac. It looks like a huge castle, but it is really a hotel. It was built in 1893 by the Canadian Pacific Railway.

Next I visited the Musée de la Civilisation. This modern museum sits along the river, near the Old Port. I learned about the history of Québec, and I did a lot of fun activities.

I'm sad to leave this beautiful city. It has been fun hearing French spoken everywhere. Next stop, Detroit, Michigan!

The Fairmont Le Château Frontenac was named after Louis de Buade, Count of Frontenac. He was the leader of New France from 1672 to 1698.

Chapter 2   Detroit, Michigan

Detroit is the oldest city in the midwestern part of the United States. I took a lot of photos there.

Detroit sits in an area that was known as le détroit. Détroit means **strait** in French. In 1701, Antoine de la Mothe Cadillac of France started a settlement there. He called it Fort Pontchartrain du Détroit. It was surrounded by high walls made of logs. The walls protected against Indian and, later, British attacks. But, after the fall of Québec City, Fort Pontchartrain also fell to the British in 1760.

The Renaissance Center in Downtown Detroit. It is a beautiful office and hotel center on East Jefferson between Randolph and Beaubien on the Detroit River. Beaubien Street is named for one of the original French family farms. Street names are almost all that is left of Detroit's French beginnings.

In 1913, Henry Ford invented the moving **assembly line** in Detroit. That made it possible to make many cars at lower prices. You didn't have to be rich to buy a car!

No trip to Detroit is complete without a visit to the Henry Ford Museum. Did you know that Detroit is nicknamed the "Motor City" and "Motown"? That's because Detroit was once where many American automobiles, or "motor cars" were made.

The Henry Ford Museum is the best place to see the history of planes, trains, automobiles, and even bicycles. You can even take a ride in a Model T, like the one in this picture.

The Motown Historical Museum is one of Detroit's most popular spots. On my visit, I was able to see where dozens of hit songs were recorded. I also saw great costumes and old photos. I even got to sing into the **echo chamber** used on many Motown hits!

Yes, Detroit was a lot of fun. But it was time to head to St. Louis.

Detroit is also the world-famous home of the "Motown Sound." It all started when Berry Gordy opened his own record company and called his headquarters "Hitsville, U.S.A." Many of the biggest African American popular music stars got their start at Motown Records.

Chapter 3   St. Louis, Missouri

In 1764, two French traders, Pierre Laclede and Auguste Chouteau, set up a fur-trading settlement where the Mississippi River meets the Missouri River. They named it St. Louis, in honor of King Louis IX of France.

In 1803, France sold the Louisiana Territory to the United States. The sale was called the Louisiana Purchase, and it included St. Louis. After that, more English-speaking people moved to the town. But St. Louis stayed mostly French for about twenty more years.

In the 1820s, St. Louis's French fur-trading families began to lose their influence. The first mayor was an English-speaking army doctor who won the election over the French-speaking candidate in 1823.

Between 1830 and 1860, the population grew by the thousands as the nation moved West. Germans, Irish, and others came to start new lives on the edge of the frontier. By the 1890s, thousands of other **immigrants** had joined them.

The 1904 World's Fair was held in St. Louis. It celebrated the 100th anniversary of the Louisiana Purchase. In seven months, about 20 million people from around the world went to the fair.

You can still visit and take pictures of some of the fair buildings that were not torn down. Speaking of pictures, here are some still pictures from the video I shot in St. Louis. I hope you like them.

Did you know

that peanut butter, hot dogs, hamburgers, iced tea, and ice cream cones were all made popular at the 1904 World's Fair? It seems like St. Louis was the place to be!

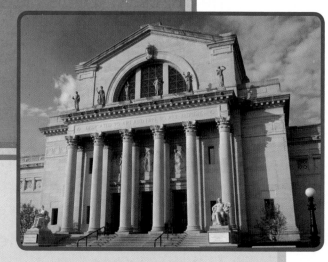

The St. Louis Art Museum is in Forest Park, the site of the 1904 World's Fair. It was one of eight "palaces" built for the fair. It was the only one that was built to be permanent.

The Gateway Arch is 630 feet wide and 630 feet tall.

St. Louis's most famous landmark is the Gateway Arch. It was built to honor all the pioneers who passed through St. Louis on their way out West.

I took a tram ride to the top of the Arch. What a view! At the bottom, I saw a great exhibit about the St. Louis riverfront in the 1800s. I also saw an exhibit about how workers put the last piece of the Arch into place in 1965.

The Arch is a part of the Jefferson National Expansion Memorial. It is a park that includes a museum that tells about America's westward growth. There is also the Old Courthouse, one of the oldest buildings in St. Louis.

I made one last stop before going on to New Orleans. I drove about an hour south of St. Louis to the town of Ste. Genevieve. It is the only French colonial village that is left in the United States. It also has the largest group of French colonial buildings in North America. More than fifty of the buildings were built before 1825!

Each spring, the **descendants** of the French settlers hold the French Heritage Festival in Ste. Genevieve to celebrate their history. In the winter, there is also the King's Ball. This celebration has been held for more than 250 years. People dress in French colonial clothing as they listen and dance to traditional music.

The Amoureaux House in Ste. Genevieve was built in 1792. French colonial settlers on the Mississippi River built homes like this, with front porches. The log walls were set directly in the earth, with no foundation.

Did you know
that New Orleans, at eight feet below sea level, is the second-lowest place in the United States? Death Valley, California, is the lowest.

Chapter 4   New Orleans, Louisiana

In 1718, the French built a colonial settlement in North America they called New Orleans. They must have known how important the Mississippi River would be, because they built the settlement right next to it.

New Orleans is the only city in the United States where French was spoken for almost 100 years. Today, the city is still full of French influences. You can see it in the music, food, buildings, and celebrations of New Orleans shown on the next pages.

15

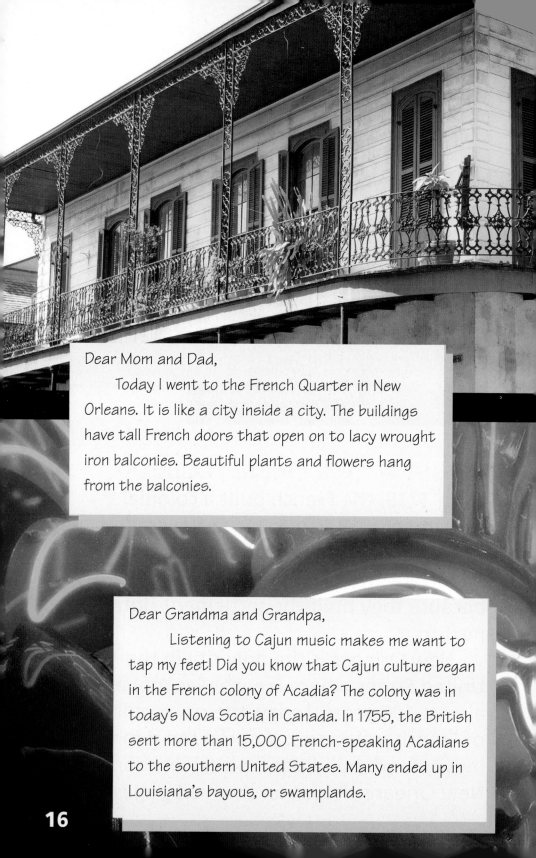

Dear Mom and Dad,

Today I went to the French Quarter in New Orleans. It is like a city inside a city. The buildings have tall French doors that open on to lacy wrought iron balconies. Beautiful plants and flowers hang from the balconies.

Dear Grandma and Grandpa,

Listening to Cajun music makes me want to tap my feet! Did you know that Cajun culture began in the French colony of Acadia? The colony was in today's Nova Scotia in Canada. In 1755, the British sent more than 15,000 French-speaking Acadians to the southern United States. Many ended up in Louisiana's bayous, or swamplands.

Purple, green, and gold are the colors of the Mardi Gras. Beads in those colors are thrown from the colorful floats. It's fun to try to catch them!

Dear Sis,

I just learned about Mardi Gras! It means "Fat Tuesday" in French. From 1699 to the mid-1700s, the French in New Orleans celebrated Mardi Gras with masked balls and parties. The parties ended when the Spanish took control of New Orleans in the 1760s.

Then in 1827, French descendants began to celebrate Mardi Gras again. Carnival, the big celebration, begins January 6 and runs for several weeks until it ends on Fat Tuesday, in late February or early March.

17

Chapter 5   Soufrière, St. Lucia

St. Lucia is an island in the Caribbean Sea. It is just twenty-seven miles long and fourteen miles wide. It has twin mountains called the Pitons and a tropical rain forest.

I stayed in Soufrière and took guided tours around the island. I asked my tour guide a lot of questions, and I recorded her answers.

Me: Tell me something about the French in St. Lucia.

Guide: Well, the French came here in 1651. For many years, they fought the English for control of the island. St. Lucia changed hands fourteen times before the French finally lost it in 1814.

Soufrière is the oldest settlement on the island of St. Lucia.

This is a plantation in St. Lucia. Many fruits and vegetables, including cocoa, bananas, mangoes, and coconuts, are grown on these big farms.

Me: Are there any French influences today?

Guide: Oh, yes! Although not many French people settled here, the French culture is everywhere. You can see it in the food, place names, surnames, music, dance, and island *patois*. That's the local language that is spoken here, along with English. However, the strongest traditions in St. Lucian culture today are African.

Me: Is there anything to see from the old days?

Guide: Yes, we'll be visiting the Fond Doux Estate. It is one of the first farms set up by the French on St. Lucia. You'll see the "cocoa dance." Workers dance on the cocoa beans to make them easier to peel before they are shipped to the chocolate factory.

The next day we took a bus to the rain forest. It was on the other side of the island.

Me: There are so many beautiful plants, flowers, trees, and fruits here. I also hear a lot of birds, but where are they?

Guide: They are way, way up over your head. They live in the thick growth of the high trees. If you use your binoculars, you might see the brightly colored St. Lucia Parrot. We call it the "Jacquot."

Wow! The rain forest was amazing! I really liked St. Lucia. It is a mix of the many cultures. You might dine at an Indian restaurant in a French-named town, then visit a British fort— all on the same day.

St. Lucia Parrots are rare. You can find them only in St. Lucia.

Summary

That was quite a trip, wasn't it? I never realized how much France has left its mark on different places in North America.

You have read about people from France who long ago settled in many areas of North America. You have also learned some facts about those French settlements as they are today.

Do a little research on your own. Find out what groups of people have lived in your area over the past 500 years. Where did they come from? What parts of their culture did they bring with them? Is there anything from those cultures that is still in your area today? It might be fun to find out!

Over the years, the French have continued to affect American culture in art, fashion, and cooking. The Statue of Liberty in New York City was a gift from France to honor the years of friendship between our two countries.

Now Try This

Thinking About the Future

You have seen how the French influenced culture in North America. Now think about where you live. How are you and your neighbors affecting the world around you?

Several hundred years from now, people will look back to study the people who lived where you live today. They will have a lot of questions: What music, art, and writing did they create? What buildings did they put up or tear down? What birds, animals, and natural places did they preserve or destroy?

To answer those questions, you might want to identify the important things in your community that tell about your culture and should be preserved.

Brownstone buildings like these are protected in some communities by laws that make it illegal to destroy or change them.

1. First, make a list of things where you live that you want to see preserved for the future. Your list might include art, buildings, events, or items from the natural world.

2. Choose two items from your list. Make a plan for how these two items might be preserved for several hundred years. What will the items need to be protected from? How might the items be protected? Whose help will be needed to protect them?

3. Draw a picture of someone looking at one of the items hundreds of years from now. What do you think that person might say about what he or she is seeing? Write it at the bottom of your picture.

4. What would you like to tell the person in the picture about the item? Write a paragraph that explains why the item was worth preserving.

Glossary

assembly line *n.* a row of workers and machines along which work is passed until the final product is made.

bilingual *adj.* able to speak two languages.

descendants *n.* people related to a person or persons who lived in the past.

echo chamber *n.* a room or space with walls that reflect sound so that an echo sound effect is made.

fortified *adj.* made stronger against attack.

immigrants *n.* people who come from somewhere else to live in a country permanently.

influence *n.* effect on someone or something.

strait *n.* a narrower strip of water that connects two larger bodies of water.